Faith
&
Worship

Look for these topics in the Everyday Matters Bible Studies for Women

Acceptance	Mentoring
Bible Study & Meditation	Outreach
Celebration	Prayer
Community	Reconciliation
Confession	Sabbath & Rest
Contemplation	Service
Faith	Silence
Fasting	Simplicity
Forgiveness	Solitude
Gratitude	Stewardship
Hospitality	Submission
Justice	Worship

Faith
&
Worship

Spiritual Practices
FOR EVERYDAY LIFE

HENDRICKSON
PUBLISHERS

**Everyday Matters Bible Studies for Women—
Faith & Worship**

© 2014 Hendrickson Publishers Marketing, LLC
P. O. Box 3473
Peabody, Massachusetts 01961-3473
www.hendrickson.com

ISBN 978-1-61970-437-4

Printed in the United States of America

Contents

Everyday Matters Bible Studies for Women

Worship

Holy Habits

Spiritual Practices for Everyday Life

Everyday life today is busier and more distracting than it has ever been before. While cell phones and texting make it easier to keep track of children and each other, they also make it harder to get away from the demands that overwhelm us. Time, it seems, is a shrinking commodity. But God, the Creator of time, has given us the keys to leading a life that may be challenging but not overwhelming. In fact, he offers us tools to do what seems impossible and come away refreshed and renewed. These tools are called spiritual practices, or spiritual disciplines.

Spiritual practices are holy habits. They are rooted in God's word, and they go back to creation itself. God has hardwired us to thrive when we obey him, even when it seems like his instructions defy our "common sense." When we engage in the holy habits that God has ordained, time takes on a new dimension. What seems impossible is actually easy; it's easy because we are tapping into God's resources.

The holy habits that we call spiritual practices are all geared to position us in a place where we can allow the Holy Spirit to work in us and through us, to grant us power and strength to do the things we can't do on our own. They take us to a place where we can become intimate with God.

While holy habits and everyday life may sound like opposites, they really aren't.

As you learn to incorporate spiritual practices into your life, you'll find that everyday life is easier. At the same time, you will draw closer to God and come to a place where you can luxuriate in his rich blessings. Here is a simple example. Elizabeth Collings hated running household errands. Picking up dry cleaning, doing the grocery shopping, and chauffeuring her kids felt like a never-ending litany of menial chores. One day she had a simple realization that changed her life. That day she began to use her "chore time" as a time of prayer and fellowship with God.

Whenever Elizabeth walked the aisle of the supermarket, she prayed for each person who would eat the item of food she selected. On her way to pick up her children, she would lay their lives out before God, asking him to be there for them even when she couldn't. Each errand became an opportunity for fellowship with God. The chore that had been so tedious became a precious part of her routine that she cherished.

The purpose of these study guides is to help you use spiritual practices to make your own life richer, fuller, and deeper. The series includes twenty-four spiritual practices that are the building blocks of Christian spiritual formation. Each practice is a holy habit that has been modeled for us in the Bible. The practices are acceptance, Bible study and meditation, celebration, community, confession, contemplation, faith, fasting, forgiveness, gratitude, hospitality, justice, mentoring, outreach, prayer, reconciliation, Sabbath and rest, service, silence, simplicity, solitude, stewardship, submission, and worship.

As you move through the practices that you select, remember Christ's promise in Matthew 11:28–30:

> *Come to me, all of you who are weary and carry heavy burdens. Take my yoke upon you. Let me teach you, because I am humble and gentle at heart, and you will find rest for your souls. For my yoke is easy to bear, and the burden I give you is light.*

Introduction

to the Practice of Faith & Worship

You've probably heard the saying, "That's why they call it faith." People tend to say this to someone facing a dilemma where none of the options seem to be clearly directed. But in this saying, have you ever wondered who "they" are and what "it" is?

It is safe to assume that "they" are those who have made a decision—without clear assurances of the outcome—and have done so in faith. And "it"? So small a word that carries so many possibilities. "It" could be the decision to uproot the family and relocate; "it" might be the moment of realization that it's time to remove oneself from an abusive relationship. "It" could be the hope vested in a major career move, or in the decision to forego a career. Regardless, "it"—for the follower of Jesus—never stands in isolation from the faith that undergirds it.

There is a scenario one could imagine of an unbeliever trying to grasp God's eternal plan of salvation:

The skeptic asks a believer, "You mean to tell me that God chose to place his Son in a remote spot on earth at a time where there was no modern means of travel or communications?"

"Yes," the believer answers.

"And the Son of God chose a dozen uneducated fishermen and laborers to spread the word around the world?"

"Yes," again is the response.

"And somehow this is supposed to be believed by people for thousands of years to come?"

Again, "Yes."

The skeptic says, "I hope God had a backup plan."

The walk of people of faith is God's only backup plan. We take the gospel on faith, and as our faith is supported by experience, it grows. But it is always a matter of stepping out into the unknown, simply trusting that God is provident, loving, and faithful. Yet somehow, when we are confronted by something we care about desperately, it often feels like we are stepping out in faith for the first time. Walking in faith is tricky stuff; God doesn't give us backup plans.

In this first study, we will explore the challenges of acting on faith, making life decisions based on an invisible reality. We will also examine that unique place of safety and resolve that asserts itself in the soul of a believer who, though sometimes blind and other times confused, chooses the sure path of faith and steps onto it confidently. Be strong in faith. Go forth with confidence—not in your circumstances, but in the God who has promised to direct your path.

The second study focuses on worship. Often we tend to associate worship with the event related to Sunday morning in a particular locale. Yet consider what worship might look like if was stripped of this cultural association with Sunday mornings and instead found expression in the everyday moments of your daily life. A missionary once said, "Our work is our prayer." Let's replace the word "prayer" with the word "worship" and proclaim that "our work is our worship."

Seeing daily life through this lens brings new dimension and vitality to your sense of purpose and mission—to your vocation, or calling, in life. In fact, not only should our work be seen as our worship, but all manner of motions we exert day in and day out are assertions of praise to God for life and vocation. Whether it be through practicing law or medicine, waiting on tables, managing or assisting in an office or business, teaching, writing a book, baking homemade bread, cleaning your house (or someone else's), homeschooling your children, sitting in traffic, or going to the gym or grocery store, the practice of worship happens every day. In this study, we will explore the many facets of worship and how women of faith can appropriate the practice in their daily lives. We examine the ways in which worship is multidimensional, creative, individual, and holy. Let's tune our hearts to be implements of worship in *all* that we do, *wherever* we are.

Faith

CHAPTER 1

Faith

I'll See It When I Believe It

> Faith is the confidence that what we
> hope for will actually happen; it gives us
> assurance about things we cannot see.
>
> HEBREWS 11:1

For this study, read Hebrews 11:1–12:2.

While the Epistle to the Hebrews was written over two thousand years ago, there still exists no better definition of faith than the one found in this book. Faith is a confidence and a hope that something will happen—even an assurance of it—despite the fact that we cannot see or know how our hope will be fulfilled. It is belief in the face of no supporting evidence. It is the belief that God will keep his promises.

After defining faith, the author of Hebrews lists a "Who's Who" of the Old Testament: people whose faith was great, in many cases epic. The first person mentioned is Abel—not one of the first people who usually come to mind when we think of biblical giants of faith. But his act of faith, which many would call obedience, placed him at the top of this list. Abel believed that God knew what he wanted in an offering, and Abel didn't try to second-guess God.

Abraham is mentioned three times in this account of giants of faith. First, we read that God called him to leave his home, family, and country, promising him an eternal inheritance. Next, we are reminded of Abraham's and Sarah's faith that God would give them a child despite their age and condition. Lastly, we hear about Abraham's faith and obedience when God told him to sacrifice Isaac, the very son through whom his descendants would come. Any one of these displays of faith would be out of the ordinary; for one person to be challenged that way three times and to maintain steadfast faith is *extra*ordinary.

Moses' faith is also mentioned three times. The Israelites' crossing of the Red Sea and their march around the walls of Jericho make the list, as do Noah, Rahab, Gideon, Samson, David, Samuel, and the prophets. "How much more do I need to say?" the author asks (v. 32). While these members of this "Hall of Faith" are an impressive group, it is reassuring to remember that they were also very human; they had failed many times in many ways. In a fit of anger, Moses killed a man; David had an innocent man killed in order to steal his wife; and Samson let his bedazzlement of Delilah bring him to ruin.

And there are instances in the New Testament as well: Peter denying—not once but three times!—that he even knew Jesus, and Thomas—who will always be known as "Doubting Thomas"—being embarrassed shortly after saying to the other apostles that he wouldn't believe Jesus had really risen from the dead unless he saw "the nail wounds in his hands, put [his] fingers into them, and [placed his] hand into the wound in his side" (John 20:24–29). But Jesus reinstates Peter by asking him three times, "Peter, do you love me?" And he appears to Thomas, saying, "Don't be faithless any longer. Believe!" To which Thomas exclaims: "My Lord and my God!" Apparently, what we've done wrong or how many times we've failed, however, is not what defines us in the arena of faith. God isn't keeping score.

The first two verses of Hebrews 12 give us great encouragement and specific direction for our walk of faith. The first verse tells us that "we are surrounded by . . . a huge crowd of witnesses to the life of faith." These are the very men and women named in the previous chapter, along with the rest of heaven itself. Since we are actually being cheered on by Abraham and David and Gideon and Joshua, the writer says in the first verse, "let us strip off every weight that slows us down. . . . And let us run with endurance the race God has set before us."

How? "We do this by keeping our eyes on Jesus, the champion who initiates and perfects our faith." We don't perfect our faith; he does. As Jesus said to Thomas, "You believe because you have seen me. Blessed are those who believe without seeing me."

"That man is perfect in faith who can come to God in the utter dearth of his feelings and desires, without a glow or an aspiration, with the weight of low thoughts, failures, neglects, and wandering forgetfulness, and say to Him, 'Thou art my refuge.'" —George MacDonald

> *As you study this chapter, think about your own personal "Hall of Faith"—times when you believed without seeing and watched God honor that faith. Then think about a situation you are facing now that requires believing without seeing.*

1. Why was Abel's offering accepted, while God rejected Cain's? While the biblical account doesn't tell us (see Genesis 4:2–5), theologians believe that Cain disobeyed God's instructions for making an acceptable offering, which needed to involve a blood sacrifice. Abel didn't necessarily work harder or give up more to make an acceptable sacrifice; what he did was to obey the Lord. What do you think the connection is between obedience and faith? Have you ever tried to second-guess God? What was the result?

2. Do you think it gets easier to have faith after you've experienced God delivering on his promises? Could that be why Abraham was able to trust and obey in three situations where so much was at stake? What does this say about our walk in faith?

3. Hebrews 11:13 says, "All of these people died still believ-ing what God had promised them. They did not receive what was promised, but they saw it all from a distance and welcomed it." What was it that God had promised that they didn't receive? What have we received that they didn't? What does this imply about our faith?

4. Have you struggled with the promises of God, believing and trusting while waiting, without seeing concrete results? What are those promises? How have you been able to navi-gate the troubled times of not knowing what God is doing?

5. How can you attest to God's faithfulness when all tem-poral evidence contradicts it? What is the value of looking back on past events, as the author of Hebrews did?

6. Name three areas or situations in your life in which faith demands that you believe without seeing (relationships, finances, work, social circles, and so on). Now look for Scripture that addresses similar situations. What does God say about the situation? How do your obedience and your faith reconcile with each other in that situation?

"Faith is to believe what we do not see, and the reward of faith is to see what we believe." —St. Augustine

Points to Ponder

Thomas Merton says, "You do not need to know precisely what is happening, or exactly where it is all going. What you need is to recognize the possibilities and challenges offered by the present moment, and to embrace them with courage, faith and hope."

- How can you approach your life with "courage, faith and hope"?

And A. W. Tozer writes, "If God gives you a watch, are you honoring Him more by asking Him what time it is or by simply consulting the watch?"

- What do you think he means?

- How does it relate to the matter of faith?

Prayer

Dear Lord, thank you for your unfailing patience, for being the "author and the finisher of our faith." Thank you for using imperfect people to do your will, for not giving up on us, for giving us second chances. Please grow my faith. Help me to put trust in you even when I don't feel like I can do it. Help me keep my eyes on you and your Son. Thank you that I can say to you, "I believe; help my unbelief."

Add your prayer in your own words.

Amen.

Put It into Practice

This week, in the morning when you're ready to turn on your computer, cell phone, iPad, or any electronic device, *don't*. Keep them off while you go to a quiet place, center yourself in prayer, and ask God to give you the faith you need to obey him in the coming day. Give God and God alone those first precious minutes of each new day.

Take-away Treasure

After the Israelites won a miraculous battle against their archenemy, the Philistines, Scripture records: "Samuel then took a large stone and . . . [he] named it Ebenezer (which means 'stone of help'), for he said, 'Up to this point the Lord has helped us!'" (1 Samuel 7:12). With the beloved hymn, "Come, Thou Fount of Every Blessing," likewise we should remember that "up to this point the Lord has helped us!"

> *Here I raise mine Ebenezer;*
> *hither by thy help I'm come;*
> *and I hope, by thy good pleasure,*
> *safely to arrive at home.*

CHAPTER 2

Action Required!

Stepping Out in Faith

"I promise you what I promised Moses: 'Wherever
you set foot, you will be on land I have given you.'
. . . No one will be able to stand against you as
long as you live. For I will be with you as I was
with Moses. I will not fail you or abandon you."

JOSHUA 1:3, 5

For this week's study, read Joshua 1–2 and 6.

Moses is dead, and Joshua has been assigned the mission of
leading the people of Israel onto new ground—the "promised land." Before embarking on the daunting enterprise
of crossing the Jordan River, God promises to Joshua that
his efforts will be met with favor (1:3–5). God's instructions are simple and straightforward: First, he tells Joshua,
"This is my command—be strong and courageous!" In fact,
God tells Joshua to "be strong and courageous" three times
within four verses (vv. 6–9). Next he tells Joshua, "Do not be
afraid or discouraged" (1:9).

Joshua is brand new at his job. He may well have preferred that God give him directions that were a little more specific, that God would give him a clue as to what he'd be facing in the next few days. But God simply tells him to do three things: to be strong and courageous, to obey the instructions that Moses had given, and to study and meditate upon the Scriptures day and night (1:7–9). Based on those instructions, Joshua calls together the officers of Israel to lead the people across the Jordan and to conquer the territory. The first thing he does is to send two spies into the promised land to scope out the situation.

The next chapter tells the story of Rahab, the prostitute who hid the spies. Rahab certainly didn't need any more trouble in her life. Her profession most likely put her at odds with the locals and the authorities, so why does she hide the Israelite men? Rahab tells the spies, "I know the LORD has given you this land" (Joshua 2:8–12). Rahab has put herself and her family at great risk by stepping out in faith in a God that wasn't even her God. And since her house was built into the town wall (v. 15), her home was an obvious place for the king's men to search. In fact, the king sent men directly to her house to look for the spies.

In her article "Rahab: An Unlikely Servant" in the *Everyday Matters Bible for Women*, Jonalyn Fincher imagines what it must have been like for Rahab when the spies arrived at her house. For once in her life, this prostitute had the upper hand with the men who had come to her home; it might well have been tempting to refuse to do their bidding. But this woman displays courage and faith by not only hiding them, but also lying to the king's men who have been sent to find them.

After Rahab has satisfied the king's men that the spies have already left her house, she asks the Israelite spies for protection for her and her family. They agree, and they issue a strange condition for her safety: she must leave hanging from the window the scarlet rope she used to rescue the spies (2:17–21). Once again, Rahab agrees. She doesn't say, "Are you kidding? I risk my life for you, and you tell me to leave the very rope I used to rescue you right in the window you used to escape?" It seems like the spies' condition for her safety is the last thing that would guarantee her safety. But Rahab simply agrees. Talk about faith.

This week's Scripture passage is the prelude to the famous story of another act of faith that was the utter opposite of what logic or common sense would dictate: the story of how Joshua and his men won the city of Jericho for the Israelites (Joshua 6:1–23). Talk about counterintuitive! When was the last time you heard of men conquering a city by merely marching around it, blasting horns and shouting? But that was God's plan. Joshua and his men obeyed, and they were successful.

Believing that God will keep his promises is essential to faith. But acting on that belief is equally necessary. If Joshua believed that God would give the Israelites the land but failed to step out and act on God's promises, it wouldn't have happened. If Rahab had believed that the Israelites' God would protect her, but failed to actually set the scarlet rope in her window, all bets would have been off. Faith is believing; but it is also acting upon that belief.

*"Just as the birds always find the air whenever
they fly, so wherever we go or wherever we are,
we find God present." —St. Francis de Sales*

*Steps of faith abound in this week's study. As you
begin, reflect on the relationship between obedience
and stepping out in faith. Think about times in your life
when you stepped out. Are you ready to set out again?*

1. What emotional and psychological hurdles do you think
Joshua had to overcome to assume the leadership role after
Moses died? We often aspire to leadership roles, but what
are the downsides of being a leader? What are the upsides?
Do you think a leader needs more faith than a follower?

2. Why do you think God prefaces his command to Joshua
with the words, "I promise you what I promised Moses"?
What has God promised other men and women in the Bible
that he promises you?

3. What are the promises that God has so far fulfilled in your life? How can looking back on those experiences help you as you navigate current challenges in your life?

4. Does acting on faith in this way suggest that God will give us whatever we want? If so, in what way? If not, why not?

5. How can a person maintain a vibrant faith even if the "promised land" remains beyond our reach? Have you experienced this?

6. Put yourself in Rahab's place. She didn't know the men who came to her for help, and she didn't know their God, yet she stepped out in faith in an extraordinary way. When was the first time you stepped out in faith, even when you had little or no personal experience with belief? What came out of that experience?

"Faith is taking the first step even when you don't see the whole staircase." —Martin Luther King, Jr.

Points to Ponder

C. S. Lewis said, "We're not necessarily doubting that God will do the best for us; we are wondering how painful the best will turn out to be."

- Why do you think that faith in God often involves undergoing pain?

- Can you personally relate to Lewis's quote?

Prayer

Lord, speak to us in the moment of trust and help us meet it with action. Whisper the words of promise and hope such as you gave Joshua. As we act and set our feet upon new ground, we trust that you will meet us there, open the way, and give us courage and strength to enter the land. Lord, give me the eyes to see and ears to hear your whispers of guidance. Then, having seen and heard, grant me the courage and strength to act with concrete steps. Cast from me doubts and double-mindedness. May my life be a picture of your faithfulness amid my weakness.

Add your prayer in your own words.

Amen.

Put It into Practice

Is there some place God has been nudging you toward? A friend you ought to visit or a job to apply for? As an act of will, grounded in surety, make the physical effort to execute this guidance by going forth into that situation. When you take steps toward that place, recall the words of God to Joshua when he faced an uncertain outcome: "Wherever you set foot, you will be on land I have given you."

Take-away Treasure

When you are facing a moment where you are about to take a step into uncertain territory (whether figuratively or literally), stop for a moment and repeat in your heart the promise God made to Joshua. Then step into the moment with your head high and in complete trust. Remember what Blaise Pascal says: "Faith is a sounder guide than reason. Reason can only go so far, but faith has no limits."

CHAPTER 3

On The Path

Just Enough Light

"You know the way to where I am going."

JOHN 14:4

For this week's study, read John 13:31–14.

In "Untidy, Mysterious Faith," her article in the *Everyday Matters Bible for Women*, Carolyn Arends refers to a story about a missionary who got lost in the jungle. He made his way to a village and asked one of the men there to lead him out. The man agreed and for an hour he walked ahead of the missionary, clearing a way through the thick foliage with a machete. Eventually the missionary asked, "Are you sure we're going the right way? Isn't there a path somewhere?" The villager smiled and replied, "Friend, I *am* the path."

In this week's Scripture, Jesus says, "I am the way, the truth, and the life. No one can come to the Father except through me" (14:6). Jesus *is* the path.

He is preparing his disciples for the events that will soon follow: he will be betrayed, arrested, and crucified. He

23

wants his followers to know that even though soon he won't be with them, their hearts should not be troubled; that he and the Father will take care of them; that he will send the Holy Spirit "who leads into all truth" (14:17). Later he says, "I am leaving you with a gift—peace of mind and heart. And the peace I give is a gift the world cannot give. So don't be troubled or afraid" (14:27). It has been said that fear is the opposite of faith. It's easy to be fearful when we don't know where the path leads—or even where to plant our foot in the next step. But Jesus is the way, the truth, and the life. That is the path we are on.

Carolyn Arends ends her article repeating Jesus' words, "I am the way": "My ideas about God are not the path. My church tradition, helpful as it is in pointing to him, is not the path. Only God is. Only he can lead me through the jungle that is my life and into the boundless adventure of life with him."

In Psalm 119:105, the writer proclaims, "Your word is a lamp to guide my feet and a light for my path." In ancient Israel, oil lamps were the only source of lamplight. As you can imagine, the small flame ignited did not shed light further than just a few inches ahead. While most of us would like a powerful spotlight that would let us see far ahead in life, God has seen fit to instruct us to follow him step by step, seeing just a few inches in front of us. Knowing that he is the path and his word is the lamp, we can take life one step at a time with the assurance that he will never leave us nor forsake us, that our faith is like light or manna. We need only a little at a time.

> "We spend time worrying about our kids' faith
> when the greatest influence in their lives is
> you sticking to yours." —Mark Holmen

As you study this chapter, set a candle before you and light it. Thank God for his direction in your life, one small step at a time.

1. Why do you think Jesus is described in metaphors so much in the Gospels? What are some other metaphors (for example, "the vine") used in describing him? What do those metaphors have in common? What are some differences between them?

shepherd
living water

2. In John 14:4, Jesus says, "You know the way to where I am going." Just before that, he tells his disciples that he's going to prepare a place for them. What do you think the disciples thought he meant? Why did he tell them that they knew "the way to where"? Why do you think he didn't just tell him the answer outright?

3. If you were to speak to your loved ones before your death and promise them something upon your departure, what would you want to give them? Why did Jesus choose to leave the disciples with peace of mind and heart? What is the difference between peace of mind and peace of heart?

4. Like the missionary in the jungle who followed the man with the machete, have you ever felt surrounded solely by tangles and obstacles on your path? Name an instance in your life where you followed God step by step in the middle of your own personal jungle? What were some of your experiences along the way?

5. Carolyn Arends points out that neither her church nor her personal ideas are the path in the walk of faith. What are some of the pitfalls of thinking that our communities of faith or tenets of theology are "the path"?

6. In the last half of John 14, Jesus promises that he will send the Holy Spirit, "who leads into all truth." In verse 26, Jesus says, "But when the Father sends the Advocate as my representative—that is, the Holy Spirit—he will teach you everything and will remind you of everything I have told you." Why does Jesus refer to the Holy Spirit as the "Advocate"? What does that mean? How does the Holy Spirit work in your life?

"If God sends us on hard paths, he provides us with strong shoes." —Corrie ten Boom

Points to Ponder

Corrie ten Boom has said, "When a train goes through a tunnel and it gets dark, you don't throw away the ticket and jump off. You sit still and trust the engineer."

- Do you always need to be in the driver's seat?

• Is there fear in your life today that is giving the enemy an unnecessary advantage?

Prayer

My Lord God, I have no idea where I am going. I do not see the road ahead of me. I cannot know for certain where it will end. Nor do I really know myself, and the fact that I think that I am following your will does not mean that I am actually doing so. But I believe that the desire to please you does in fact please you. I hope that I will never do anything apart from that desire. Therefore will I trust you always, though I may seem to be lost and in the shadow of death. I will not fear, for you are ever with me, and you will never leave me to face my perils alone. —Thomas Merton, *Thoughts in Solitude*

Add your prayer in your own words.

Amen.

Put It into Practice

Remember that Jesus gave us a "going away gift": peace of mind and heart. If you are feeling anxious today, ask Jesus for that gift. Pray: "Lord, help me to listen to you in prayer as much as you listen to me." Don't just look for the path. Listen.

Take-away Treasure

In "Dark Nights of the Soul" in the *Everyday Matters Bible for Women*, Sally Morgenthaler encourages us to embrace the dark times that challenge our faith, when we can't seem to see that path before us:

> *My usual response to the dark is to switch on the biggest spotlight I can find. But perhaps true transformation requires periods of darkness; perhaps it takes place even in dim and murky places. Read only a few of the psalms, and you see this theme played out: disorientation and doubt are gestational to faith. Consider the trust displayed by the downcast and disturbed soul in Psalm 42:3–5. Enveloped in a seemingly infinite expanse of questions, the uncertain pilgrim stretches forward to know and see beyond himself.*

CHAPTER 4

KISS

Keep it Simple, Sister

"And if God cares so wonderfully for wildflowers that are here today and thrown into the fire tomorrow, he will certainly care for you. Why do you have so little faith?"

MATTHEW 6:30

For this study, read Matthew 6:9–34.

Twenty years ago, e-mail was virtually unknown. Cell phones, texting, Google, and Facebook didn't exist. Jobs were more plentiful; the economy was better. Whether it's true or not, it seems that life was simpler then. But maybe not. Maybe life has never been simple. In the Sermon on the Mount, Christ lays out a blueprint for his followers of how to live. He urges them not to store up treasures here on earth but rather in heaven. After all, there's no chance of losing heavenly treasures; they won't rust away or get stolen. Then he tells them not to worry (vv. 26–29):

*Look at the birds. They don't plant or harvest or store food in
barns, for your heavenly Father feeds them. And aren't you
far more valuable to him than they are? Can all your worries
add a single moment to your life? And why worry about your
clothing? Look at the lilies of the field and how they grow.
They don't work or make their clothing, yet Solomon in all his
glory was not dressed as beautifully as they are.*

"Why do you have so little faith?" he asks.

Finally, he says, "So don't worry about these things, saying,
'What will we eat? What will we drink? What will we wear?'
These things dominate the thoughts of unbelievers, but
your heavenly Father already knows all your needs. Seek the
Kingdom of God above all else, and live righteously, and he
will give you everything you need" (vv. 31–33). Jesus is telling them—and us—to keep it simple.

As Keri Wyatt Kent writes in "Worry versus Faith" in the
Everyday Matters Bible for Women:

*With this simple directive, "I tell you not to worry . . ." (Mat-
thew 6:25), Jesus calls us to trust him. To do so requires
a certain emotional detachment, a conscious letting go of
needing to control the outcome of every situation. Trust is a
choice, the alternative to worry. It's not that we don't care; we
do! But we intentionally "give all [our] worries and cares to
God" (1 Peter 5:7), choosing to turn over our lives to him, one
moment at a time.*

When the disciples asked Jesus, "Who is the greatest in the
Kingdom of Heaven?" he "called a little child to him . . . then
he said, 'I tell you the truth, unless you turn from your sins

and become like little children, you will never get into the Kingdom of Heaven. So anyone who becomes as humble as this little child is the greatest in the Kingdom of Heaven'" (Matthew 18:1–4).

It appears that in Jesus' eyes, simplicity is the key—simple as a little child. With simple faith, Christ tells us, mountains can be moved. With simple faith that confuses scholars and wise men, salvation occurs. So keep it simple, sister.

"Don't tell God how big your storm is; tell the storm how big your God is." —Author unknown

As you study this chapter, think about the things that are worrying you. Do you think they're things a child would worry about? Does God want you to?

1. Jesus taught us to start our prayer by addressing God as "Abba" Father (Matthew 6:9). A more accurate translation of the word "Abba" is *Daddy*. Why do you think he used that particular word? What qualities do you think of when you think of a "daddy"?

2. What does Jesus mean by "seek the Kingdom of God above all else"? What does that look like on a day-to-day basis? What are the "all else" things in your life?

3. Think about Matthew 6:19–24. What is the connection between Jesus' words about storing up treasures (19–21) and his discussion of light and darkness (22–24)?

4. What does Jesus mean when he says that "your eye is a lamp that provides light for your body" (Matthew 6:22)? Why is this analogy mentioned in a warning about money and possessions and serving "two masters" (v. 24)?

5. In Matthew 6:34, Jesus says, "So don't worry about tomorrow, for tomorrow will bring its own worries. Today's trouble is enough for today." What if you worried about the things you had to face today? Try it for one day and share your observations with the other Bible study members when you next meet.

6. How might the promise of God taking care of us, even more so than the care he gives the flowers, be understood by someone who has suffered greatly physically or emotionally and feels bereft of this kind of watch care?

"But Jesus said, 'Let the little children come to me.
Don't stop them! For the Kingdom of Heaven belongs to
those who are like these children.'" (Matthew 19:14)

Points to Ponder

Read and think about Philippians 4:6–7: "Don't worry about anything; instead, pray about everything. Tell God what you need, and thank him for all he has done. Then you will experience God's peace, which exceeds anything we can understand. His peace will guard your hearts and minds as you live in Christ Jesus."

- If you're worried about something, have you prayed about it?

- If you've prayed about it, why are you still worried?

Prayer

Lord, sometimes the complexities of life confuse and overwhelm me. Yet all things pertaining to you are simple and accessible. The psalmist says, "When I am afraid, I will trust in you." Give me the faith of a child who doesn't question but simply believes. Help me to see you as my "Abba Father."

Add your prayer in your own words.

Amen.

Put It into Practice

This week, place a flower in a vase and set it where you spend your personal time with God. At the end of each day, write down the ongoing fears and uncertainty you are experiencing. Then, in the writing, give them to God in faith. Let the flower serve as a visible reminder of his promise to care for you even more than he does the flowers.

Take-away Treasure

O LORD, what a variety of things you have made!
    In wisdom you have made them all.
    The earth is full of your creatures.
Here is the ocean, vast and wide,
    teeming with life of every kind,
    both large and small.
See the ships sailing along,
    and Leviathan, which you made to play in the sea.
They all depend on you
    to give them food as they need it.
When you supply it, they gather it.
    You open your hand to feed them,
    and they are richly satisfied. (Psalm 104:24–28)

Notes / Prayer Requests

Notes / Prayer Requests

_____

_____

_____

_____

_____

_____

_____

_____

_____

_____

_____

_____

_____

_____

_____

_____

_____

_____

_____

_____

Worship

CHAPTER 1

God-Struck

It's All about Him

"I was dancing before the LORD, who chose
me above your father and all his family! He
appointed me as the leader of Israel, the people
of the LORD, so I celebrate before the LORD. Yes,
and I am willing to look even more foolish than
this, even to be humiliated in my own eyes!"

2 SAMUEL 6:21-22

For this study, read 2 Samuel 6:12–7:29.

In "Dance of the God-Struck" in the *Everyday Matters
Bible for Women*, Mark Buchanan describes the story of
King David moving the ark of the covenant to Jerusalem to
make a statement to the nations that "God is king in this
kingdom, lord of this land. The king acknowledges the King
beyond him, above him, to whom he owes all fealty." It is
not a political gesture but an act of worship, says Buchanan:
"So David brings the ark to Jerusalem—and he dances in
worship. Choreographed by yearning and wonder, this is
the dance of the God-struck, the God-smitten."

Think about a time when you were utterly smitten with someone—perhaps your first crush or when you first fell in love. It's a feeling like no other; that person dominates your thoughts and feelings. That is how David felt about God. He had abandoned every thought of himself and was utterly immersed in God. He was God-struck.

Scripture tells us that "David and all the people of Israel brought up the Ark of the LORD with shouts of joy and the blowing of rams' horns" (6:15). Michal, David's wife and King Saul's daughter, watches from her window. David makes sacrifices to the Lord and then blesses the people in the name of "the LORD of Heaven's Armies" (6:18). Then he gives every person there gifts of bread and cakes. Finally David goes home to bless his own family, but Michal comes out to meet him and says "in disgust, 'How distinguished the king of Israel looked today, shamelessly exposing himself to the servant girls like any vulgar person might do!'" (6:20).

Buchanan observes, "Michal seems to believe that the chief end of humanity is to uphold its own reputation. Religion is fine, in its place. But worship? Worship is a dicey thing, because modesty and moderation are Michal's watchwords, and worship always threatens them, always wants to push beyond them." True worship takes us outside of ourselves. It moves our stubborn egos aside and puts God at the center.

In "Deborah: Recognizing the True Object of Worship" in the *Everyday Matters Bible for Women*, Joy-Elizabeth Lawrence says, "Worship is about God, not us. In her book *Reaching Out without Dumbing Down*, theologian Marva Dawn writes about the importance of God being both the *subject* and *object* in our worship: 'The gifts of worship flow from God the subject and return to God as the object of our reverence.'" If we focus on who God truly is, we can't help but dance—or fall face down—in worship. He is eternal, holy, unchanging, infinite, all-powerful, all-knowing, all-wise, everywhere-present. He is gracious, merciful, and just. He is the Subject and the Object. He is Love.

True worship involves every fiber of our being. In Luke 10:25–28, an expert in religious law asks Jesus what he must do to inherit eternal life. Jesus responds by asking him what the law of Moses says, to which the man correctly answers: "'You must love the Lord your God with all your heart, all your soul, all your strength, and all your mind.' And, 'Love your neighbor as yourself.'" To God, worship is a holistic experience that includes our minds as well as our hearts and souls. And we also love him by loving one another.

David knew this and was "God-struck." He rejoiced before the ark of the Lord as God's Presence moved into the heart of David's kingdom. True worship immerses us so deeply that, like David, we forget about how we look to others.

"The message of the cross is foolish to those who are headed for destruction! But we who are being saved know it is the very power of God." (1 Corinthians 1:18)

> **As you study this chapter, think about your own particular way of worship and if it engages your heart, your mind, your soul, your strength.**

1. Were all of David's actions in the Samuel passage forms of worship? Can you think of modern-day counterparts in worship? What does giving away food have to do with worship?

2. When Michal scolded David for "acting foolishly," David gave her a strong reply (vv. 21–22). What forms of worship today appear foolish in the eyes of others? Are you willing to look foolish in your own worship? Can you find other Scriptures that discuss the foolishness of believers?

3. Are there ways of worshiping that you haven't participated in because you were self-conscious? Are there other forms of worship you might engage in?

4. In chapter 7, David realizes that while he is living in a great palace, the ark of God is "out there in a tent" (v. 2). The prophet Nathan tells David, "The LORD declares that he will make a house for you—a dynasty of kings!" (v. 11). He promises David that his house, kingdom, and throne will be secure forever. Why do you think God responds that way to David?

5. In his article, Mark Buchanan says that David's desire to move the ark to Jerusalem was not primarily a political gesture to indicate his prominence as king; it was primarily an act of worship. How was that an act of worship? What message did it send to the people in and outside of David's kingdom?

6. Does your worship service involve your intellect? Do you have a pastor who, as Paul would say, gives you "meat" and not "milk"? Do you pay attention to the words in the hymns or liturgy? What do they mean to you?

"Wonder is the basis of worship." —Thomas Carlyle

Points to Ponder

Carolyn Arends in "Flipping Worship on Its Head" in the *Everyday Matters Bible for Women* writes:

> *At the foundation of our faith is the understanding that God is triune—he's always been in relationship with himself: Father, Son, and Holy Spirit (2 Corinthians 13:14; Ephesians 2:18; 1 Peter 1:1–2). It's a divine, eternal dance among Father, Son, and Holy Spirit—loving one another, sharing mutual affection and admiration, sharing beauty and truth. Worship means realizing that, through Christ's forgiveness, we're part of that mutual fellowship with our Trinitarian God. Worship is about saying yes to that miraculous inclusion.*

- What does it mean to you when we sing to or pray in the name of the Father, the Son, and the Holy Spirit?

- Do you shy away from the doctrines handed down to us through the centuries, or do you see them as precious gifts from God to his church?

Prayer

Dear Father, I pray that you'll keep me from being judgmental like Michal. Make me willing to "look like a fool" if it pleases you, just like King David. Forgive me for thinking of how others might see me instead of focusing on you. Remind me of the indignities that Jesus suffered throughout his life and in death. Thank you, God, for your great love to me. Let me worship you—let me love you truly—with all of my heart, my soul, my mind, and with all my strength.

Add your prayer in your own words.

Amen.

Put It into Practice

Read or recite the Apostles' Creed and then the Nicene Creed. Meditate on them and praise God for his wondrous revelation of who he truly is. Here is the Apostles' Creed, believed to have been written by the apostles themselves:

> *I believe in God, the Father almighty, Creator of heaven and earth, and in Jesus Christ, his only Son, our Lord, who was conceived by the Holy Spirit, born of the Virgin Mary, suffered under Pontius Pilate, was crucified, died and was buried; he descended into hell; on the third day he rose again from the*

dead; he ascended into heaven, and is seated at the right hand
of God the Father almighty; from there he will come to judge
the living and the dead. I believe in the Holy Spirit, the holy
catholic [that is, universal] Church, the communion of saints,
the forgiveness of sins, the resurrection of the body, and
life everlasting. Amen.

Take-away Treasure

In "Worshiping with Your Heart and Mind" in the *Everyday
Matters Bible for Women,* Pam Howell and John Ortberg
encourage us toward true worship of God:

> In our day—when the beauty of liturgical traditions, the free-
> dom of charismatic expression, and the intellectual rigor of the
> Reformation are being cross-fertilized—we have a wonder-
> ful opportunity to pursue worship that balances intellect and
> passion. We can . . . step into worship fully engaged, using
> both our hearts and our minds. . . . The single most impor-
> tant aspect of balanced worship is to fully devote both your
> intellect and your emotions in your focus on God. When this
> happens, moments will come when you feel and understand
> God in ways no one could have planned.

CHAPTER 2

Weekday Worship

How to Make It a 24/7 Affair

> "For God is spirit, so those who worship
> him must worship in spirit and in truth."
>
> JOHN 4:24

For this study, read John 4.

Have you ever wished that Jesus had been more specific about how we are to worship?

In the Old Testament, God gave elaborate instructions on how he was to be worshiped. In fact, such instructions fill half the book of Exodus and the entire book of Leviticus. Everything from criteria for a perfect animal sacrifice to the fabric and construction of the priests' garments was described in detail and to be obeyed. Many of the psalms are magnificent expressions of and meditations on worship. And of course, there are stories about worship ranging from Cain and Abel, Abraham, Moses, and the building of the tabernacle, to Daniel, and the prophets, to name just a few.

In the New Testament, guidance concerning worship becomes much sparser. Jesus gives the disciples the Lord's Prayer, and he institutes the Eucharist just before his betrayal. But for the most part, Jesus does not tell us how to worship the Father. In fact, he's often criticized by the authorities for breaking the Sabbath and other rules of worship. In his encounter with the Samaritan woman, he speaks of worship and says, "God is spirit, so those who worship him must worship in spirit and in truth" (John 4:24). Here, Jesus introduces an entirely new way of worshiping God. And he refuses to lay it out in the form of rules and instructions. Instead he uses terms such as "in spirit" and "in truth." This new approach to worship is freeing but also more challenging. How do we actually *do* that? Here are a few ways:

- *Prayer.* Are you "God-struck" when you pray? How much of your prayer is about you, and how much is about God?

- *Bible reading.* In order to worship him in truth, we need to know the truth about who he is. We meet God in the Scriptures.

- *Sharing your faith.* Do you ever "brag on God"? Let others know what he's doing in your life.

- *Serving others.* When you do anything to "the least of them," you're worshiping God as well.

- *Surrender.* Turn over areas of your life to God that you haven't committed to him before. Are there areas where you've held back, such as money or time?

> *"Worship has been misunderstood as something that arises from a feeling which 'comes upon you,' but it is vital that we understand that it is rooted in a conscious act of the will, to serve and obey the Lord Jesus Christ." —Graham Kendrick*

As you study this chapter, think about worship in your own life, not just in church but daily.

1. In John 4:10, why do you think Jesus revealed so much about himself to the woman when he often didn't want his identity as the Son of God revealed?

2. In verse 19, the woman brings up the differences in worship between Jews and Samaritans, specifically where they each worship. Why do you think she brought that up?

3. In verse 23, Jesus says, "The time is coming—indeed it's here now—when true worshipers will worship the Father in spirit and in truth." What do you think Jesus meant? Why was the time "here now"?

4. What do you think Jesus meant using the future tense when he said that true worshipers *will* worship the Father in spirit and in truth? Is our worship different now than it was in his time? How? How is it similar?

5. The book of Psalms describes more about who God is than any other book in the Bible. This week, read at least one psalm a day, meditating on the nature of God and/or worship as he is revealed in the Scriptures. Share any insights or experiences with the group at the next meeting.

6. Someone once said, "God does not have favorites, but he does have intimates." What do you think that means? How do you think worship fits into that idea?

"Worship means there is nothing required of us that cannot be done as an act of worship."
—*John MacArthur*, The Glory of Heaven

Points to Ponder

Billy Graham once said, "The highest form of worship is the worship of unselfish Christian service. The greatest form of praise is the sound of consecrated feet seeking out the lost and helpless."

- Is there a service you can provide for someone else today?

- Who are the "lost and helpless" in your life?

Prayer

Heavenly Father, I ask you to show me how to worship you not solely with my heart and mind, but also with my hands and feet, my time and resources, my whole being. Please help me to fall in love with you more deeply and want to worship you more fully in spirit and in truth.

Add your prayer in your own words.

Amen.

Put It into Practice

Ask God to show you something you can do to worship him that you hadn't previously thought of as a form of worship. Ask him to make you sensitive to the prompting of his Holy Spirit.

Share any experience you might have had with the group when you next meet.

Take-away Treasure

William Barclay said, "The true, genuine worship is when a man, through his spirit, attains friendship and intimacy with God." Remember that God wants worship from you not for his ego, but for a deeper level of intimacy with you.

> *Shout with joy to the LORD, all the earth!*
> > *Worship the LORD with gladness.*
> > *Come before him, singing with joy.*
> *Acknowledge that the LORD is God!*
> > *He made us, and we are his.*
> > *We are his people, the sheep of his pasture.*
> *Enter his gates with thanksgiving;*
> > *go into his courts with praise.*
> > *Give thanks to him and praise his name.*
> *For the LORD is good.*
> *His unfailing love continues forever,*
> *and his faithfulness continues to each generation.*
> > *(Psalm 100)*

CHAPTER 3

Come-What-May Worshipers

Worshiping When We're Suffering

> The thought of my suffering . . .
>   is bitter beyond words. . . .
> Yet I still dare to hope
>   when I remember this:
> The faithful love of the LORD never ends!
>   His mercies never cease.
> Great is his faithfulness;
>   his mercies begin afresh each morning.
>
> LAMENTATIONS 3:19, 21-23

For this study, read Lamentations 3.

How wonderful it is to worship the Lord when life is good and blessings abound. During times of joy, the sun is brighter, the call of each new day sweeter. Life is an adventure, worship feels like a privilege, and God is good. Would that life were like this all the time. It is easiest to worship when we're feeling joy, gratitude, relief, or contentment. But few, if any, of us escape the times when life is a burden and sadness abounds. Innocents suffer; hardworking breadwinners lose their jobs; illness strikes during the prime of life; a husband dies. When there seems to be no good reason for the suffering, worship often feels impossible; God seems unresponsive and far away. How do we worship then?

In her article "Worship during Suffering" in the *Everyday Matters Bible for Women*, Caryn Rivadeneira talks about "come-what-may" worship. It is the same worship practiced by David and Daniel, Jeremiah and Job, and so many giants of the faith. "Even battling bitterness," says Rivadeneira, "Jeremiah dared to hope in the goodness and faithfulness of God. Even in his pain, Jeremiah experienced the joy of one of the most important truths we can grasp—that God's faithfulness never ends, no matter how things seem to us."

Corrie ten Boom is a modern-day giant of the faith. She and her family of Dutch Christians risked their lives to help Jews escape the Nazis. The ten Booms were arrested and sent to Hitler's concentration camps to suffer unspeakable acts of horror. In *The Hiding Place*, her autobiography, ten Boom says, "You can never know that Christ is all you need until Christ is all you have."

Why we have to suffer is a mystery that won't be answered in this life. But ten Boom sheds light on the mystery. When contentment, ease, health, and happiness are ours, it's easy to forget that Christ is all we need. When illness, suffering, and tragedy strike, we can't help but remember that Christ is all we need.

Pastor Rick Warren, himself no stranger to devastating sorrow, has said, "Your most profound and intimate experiences of worship will likely be your darkest days—when your heart is broken, when you feel abandoned, when you're out of options, when the pain is great—and you turn to God alone."

Throughout the Old Testament, God required sacrifice before worship, and in the New Testament, he provided the perfect sacrifice in the form of Jesus. St. Paul reminded the Roman believers that God didn't spare even his own son, but delivered him up for us all (Romans 8:32).

Remembering that puts suffering in a different light. If God allowed his own son to suffer indignity, persecution, torture, and death, who are we to demand that we be spared? We often say, "Why me?" But perhaps the more appropriate question is, "Why not me?"

Worship is the acknowledgement and the affirmation that God is provident, all loving and all merciful, not just in good times, but in all times. In her article, Caryn Rivadeneira observes that Jeremiah chose to be a come-what-may worshiper; he chose to worship God in every situation.

"Real faith is holding blessings in one hand and suffering in the other, and trusting God to use both to accomplish His will." —Ben Dailey

> *As you study this chapter, think about the times you have worshiped during suffering or watched others do so. Did you observe any redemption through or following that time of suffering? Did your worship consist of anything other than words or songs?*

1. In Lamentations 3:1–19, how many examples of his suffering does Jeremiah list? Write a list of what you are suffering right now. How does it stack up against Jeremiah's? Now read verses 20–22 out loud.

2. Jeremiah says in verse 20, "I will never forget this awful time, as I grieve over my loss." Then he "dares to hope." Is it appropriate to continue to grieve a loss during worship?

3. Do actions comprise worship as well as words? What sorts of actions might be examples of worship during suffering?

4. In verse 32, Jeremiah says that "though [the Lord] brings grief, he also shows compassion because of the greatness of his unfailing love." Have you ever felt God's compassion while you have suffered? If you are a parent, have you ever felt compassion when your child suffered—even if you could have done something to alleviate that suffering? Does that imply anything about God's compassion for us?

5. In Isaiah 48:10, God says, "I have refined you, but not as silver is refined. Rather, I have refined you in the furnace of suffering." What is (or was) your own furnace of suffering? Do you feel that your suffering purified you? How? Do you think it was worth the suffering you experienced?

6. How does the fall of Judah and Jeremiah's lament move us today to fear and love God and recognize his never-ending love for us? What should be our appropriate response to his great faithfulness?

"*Out of suffering comes the serious mind; out of salvation, the grateful heart; out of endurance, fortitude; out of deliverance, faith.*" —*John Rashin*

Points to Ponder

The practice of worship is not just to be carried out in church or with others. Personal worship creates greater intimacy with God.

• Have you worshiped God lately in his presence only?

• Have there been times when you were acutely aware of his presence? What was your response?

Prayer

Lord, it's easy to worship you in times of joy and abundance. It's much harder when I'm suffering and sad. Please show me your compassion during my times of trouble, and help me to worship you despite my circumstances.

Add your prayer in your own words.

Amen.

Put It into Practice

Use the "ACTS" form of prayer this week. When you pray:

Adore God (worship) first; then . . .
Confess whatever you need to;
Thank God for specific blessings, from his Creation to your own personal life. Finally . . .
Supplication: make your requests to him for yourself and others.

By worshiping first, your spirit will be moved as you pray further. Tell the group about your observations as you pray the ACTS this week.

Take-away Treasure

Worship is affirmation that God is God. It is not gratitude for all that happens in our lives.

We can worship God and give him glory even if we are unhappy and suffering, just like Jeremiah: "Yet I still dare to hope when I remember this: The faithful love of the LORD never ends! His mercies never cease. . . . I say to myself, 'The LORD is my inheritance; therefore, I will hope in him!'"

CHAPTER 4

How Do They Do It in Heaven?

Worshiping as Part of Eternity

> Each of these living beings had six wings, and
> their wings were covered all over with eyes,
> inside and out. Day after day and night after
> night they keep on saying, "Holy, holy, holy
> is the Lord God, the Almighty—the one who
> always was, who is, and who is still to come."
>
> REVELATION 4:8

For this study, read Revelation 4–5.

Of the entire New Testament, the theme of worship is most prominent in the book of Revelation.

We often tend to think of worship in terms of songs; in fact, many praise and worship services are solely comprised of singing. But Revelation chronicles many different elements of worship that are important for us to remember as such. These include gifts (crowns placed before the throne), incense, robes, trumpet-blowing, silence, thanksgiving, shouts of celebration, sacred meals, prostration, the laying of palm branches, silence, and all sorts of songs: hymns, doxologies, victory songs, antiphonal songs—even choruses. All of these are delivered before the throne of God. Indeed, it must take forever!

In "Seeking God in our Busyness," Priscilla Shirer's article in the *Everyday Matters Bible for Women,* she talks about the sense of guilt and failure we often experience when we think about what time with God is supposed to be like. We begin to think that we should be spending thirty minutes or an hour in prayer and worship—and how we aren't doing it. On top of that, many of us aren't even really sure what worship *is*, apart from singing and perhaps reciting some psalms. Revelation 4–5 (as well as the rest of the book) can teach us a lot about worship. And what better source? After all, this is worship in heaven.

Carolyn Arends cites Revelation 4:8–11 in her article, "Joining the Eternal Song," in the *Everyday Matters Bible for Women*. She speaks of a memory from her childhood when she first experienced an incredible moment—a beautiful sunset—in which she "had the sense that there was Something so much bigger than myself—Something that was good and true. It was that instinctive feeling in which everything in you says, *Yes!* and *Thank you!* I didn't fully understand it then, but I think everything in me was saying, *Holy!*" She notes that every time we join the beings in heaven who sing "Holy, holy, holy is the Lord God, the Almighty" we are participating in an eternal chorus—which will continue on into eternity once we are all together in the Presence of God in the New Jerusalem, when we sing:

> "*The world has now become the Kingdom of our Lord*
> *and of his Christ,*
> *and he will reign forever and ever.*" (Revelation 11:15)

But in the meantime, in life in the here and now, in the already and the not yet, does worship actually *accomplish* anything? In "Wasting Time in Worship," Marva Dawn affirms that it does:

> *As we live in worship, we're able to truly be the church for the world. Worship forms and shapes us so that, rather than trying to do church, we're able to actually be the church. . . . Worship can form me into a more generous person, because in worship I constantly see the generosity of God. Or worship can nurture and grow patience and graciousness in me as I spend time focusing on and praising God for the grace and patience he shows to me and the rest of humankind. Worship changes my perspective; it changes who I am.*

"Amen! Come, Lord Jesus! May the grace of the Lord Jesus be with God's holy people" (Revelation 22:20–21).

> *"The Kingdom of God is where we belong. It is home, and whether we realize it or not, I think we are all of us homesick for it." —Frederick Buechner*

Everyday Matters Bible Studies for Women

> **As you study this chapter, this about the times when you have sensed "Something so much bigger" than yourself and your response to that special moment.**

1. The book of Revelation makes it clear that beyond our sight there exists a host of angelic beings who actively worship God. Although what this means is outside any real human understanding, how do you see this? Does their existence comfort or challenge you?

Comfort

2. Think about the word "holy." How would you define it? Why do you think this is the word the angels summon when worshiping God? Do you see any significance in the fact that the angels repeat it three times?

without sin —
kind, giving

3. The angels celebrate the fact that God is the One who "was and is and is to come." In your own words, what does this mean?

alpha & omega

4. If you could offer worship to God by using one word three times, what would your word be?

thank you

5. Are there moments when you have strongly felt God's presence and could only respond in worship?

6. The beloved hymn "Amazing Grace" concludes: "When we've been there ten thousand years, bright shining as the sun, we've no less days to sing God's praise than when we've first begun." Think about what this means, keeping the things of this life—the joys, the heartaches—in proper perspective!

"Not until we have become humble and teachable, standing in awe of God's holiness and sovereignty, acknowledging our own littleness, distrusting our own thoughts, and willing to have our minds turned upside down, can divine wisdom become ours." —J. I. Packer

Points to Ponder

"And he also said, 'It is finished! I am the Alpha and the Omega—the Beginning and the End. To all who are thirsty I will give freely from the springs of the water of life'" (Revelation 21:6).

- What does it mean to you that Jesus is the "Alpha and Omega—the Beginning and the End"?

- How does this affect your worship now of him?

Prayer

Lord, whatever I am doing—whether relaxing or working; whether alone or in the company of others; whether
well rested or fatigued—cause me always to be mind-
ful of your intimate knowledge of my days and that you
hold my life in your hands. Help me to praise you.

Add your prayer in your own words.

Amen.

Put It into Practice

Think of one word that resounds in your heart about God
and write it down three times. Do this daily and try to find a
word you have not yet used.

Take-away Treasure

Remember that in him we live and move and have our being. This should calm our fears, mobilize us to action, and elicit our worship.

> *Christ is the visible image of the invisible God.*
>> *He existed before anything was created and is supreme*
>>> *over all creation,*
>> *for through him God created everything*
>>> *in the heavenly realms and on earth.*
>> *He made the things we can see*
>>> *and the things we can't see—*
>> *such as thrones, kingdoms, rulers, and authorities in the*
>>> *unseen world.*
>>> *Everything was created through him and for him.*
>> *He existed before anything else,*
>>> *and he holds all creation together. (Colossians 1:15–17)*

Notes / Prayer Requests

Notes / Prayer Requests

_____

_____

_____

_____

_____

_____

_____

_____

_____

_____

_____

_____

_____

_____

_____

_____

_____

Leader's Guide

to Faith & Worship

Thoughts on Where to Meet

- If you have the chance, encourage each group member to host a gathering. But make sure your host knows that you don't expect fresh baked scones from scratch or white-glove-test-worthy surroundings. Set the tone for a relaxed and open atmosphere with a warm welcome wherever you can meet. The host can provide the space and the guests can provide the goodies.

- If you can't meet in homes, consider taking at least one of your meetings on the road. Can you meet at a local place where people from your community gather? A park or a coffee shop or other public space perhaps.

- If you meet in a church space, consider partnering with another local church group and take turns hosting. How can you extend your welcome outside your group?

Thoughts on Ways to Foster Welcome

- If many of your members have a hard time meeting due to circumstances, look for ways to work around it. Consider providing childcare if there are moms who have difficulty attending, or meet in an accessible space if someone who might want to join has a disability. Does a morning time work better? Could you meet as smaller groups and then get together as a larger group for an event? Be flexible and see how you can accommodate the needs of the group. Incorporate "get to know you" activities to promote sharing. Don't take yourselves too seriously and let your humor shine through.

Incorporating Other Practices

- *Lift your voices.* Integrate worship throughout the study. Find songs that speak of faith and worship.

- *Commit to lift each other up in prayer.* You may want to have a prayer walk as part of seeing opportunities to serve in your community, or prayer partners who might be able to meet at other times.

- *Dig deep into the word.* Take the study at your own pace but consider including passages for participants to read in between meetings. The *Everyday Matters Bible for Women* has a wealth of additional resources.

- *Celebrate!* Bring cupcakes and candles, balloons or anything celebratory to distribute to each member of the group. Ask each person to share something that they want to celebrate today, be it an event, a new insight, or anything they choose.

Faith

Chapter 1: The walk of faith is a lifelong journey. At the beginning of the journey, we don't have our own scrapbook of experiences to look back on and remember how God honored our faith. Maybe that's why he gave us Hebrews 11. That chapter is a sort of scrapbook: a series of snapshots of men and women who dared to believe that God would be faithful to his promises. If the members of your group are new Christians, they may not be familiar with the stories included in this chapter. Do they know the story of Gideon? Abraham and Isaac? Moses? During your first study, ask each member of the group to find the biblical account of someone mentioned in Hebrews 11 and to be prepared to tell the group that story of faith the next time you meet. You may also want to create your own list of additional biblical characters whose stories of faith could easily have been included in the chapter. Do any members of the group have their own "snapshot" of a time when they stepped out in faith and experienced God's amazing hand in the situation? Ask them to share it with the group.

Chapter 2: What came first (of course, not in the theological sense!): the chicken or the egg? What comes first: faith or obedience? This chapter focuses on the importance of not just believing, but also acting. Consider bringing an object lesson to your meeting this week: perhaps some flour, eggs, milk, and oil. Does the group believe that mixing and heating those ingredients will result in a cake? How strongly do they believe it? Any doubt at all? Now just leave the ingredients on the table. At the end of your meeting, ask where the cake is. There's no cake, because no matter now fully we believe something, we usually need to act upon that belief in order to see the results. Believing alone is usually not enough. (This would be a good time to provide some cake for the group!)

Chapter 3: Do the members of your group remember pre-GPS times when you had to use a paper map to get to a destination? It was so easy to get lost! Getting onto the path of faith is huge, but staying on the path is a lifelong challenge. Wouldn't it be great if God gave us a GPS that would tell us every route and every turn we needed to get to our next destination? Using this analogy, we could view the Scriptures as a type of Global Positioning System rather than a road map. While a map gives us the big picture, a GPS tells us only what to do next: turn right here, go straight for one mile, and so on. Without seeing every twist and turn in advance, we have to take it on faith that we will ultimately reach our destination. Do any members of the group feel like they're lost? Remind them that unlike man's GPS, however, God will never fail us or send us in the wrong direction! "Your own ears will hear him. Right behind you a voice will say, 'This is the way you should go,' whether to the right or to the left" (Isaiah 30:21).

Chapter 4: Worrying and doing are two different things. Jesus didn't say not to fulfill our responsibilities; he said, "Don't worry." Even a child has responsibilities that need to be met. Remind your members of that difference. Then challenge them to limit their worrying to the worries of that day for seven days in a row. Next week, ask them if they learned or experienced anything new. Do they have a better sense of why Jesus said to become like little children?

Worship

Because worship truly is all about God, we tend to think of it in terms of dwelling on the psalms—"Let all that I am praise the LORD; with my whole heart, I will praise his holy name" (103:1)—praying and singing songs of worship. While those are core forms of worship, encourage your study group to think about other ways of worshiping God as you spend these next few weeks focusing on worship. How do we broaden our worship experience beyond the forms that immediately come to mind? What does Scripture teach us about worship even if the word itself doesn't challenge the members of your group—or yourself—to broaden your concepts of worship? Do individual talents foster different kinds of worship? Can the creation of art be a form of worship? Consider a project you could spend a portion of your meeting times working on together. For example, your group could make a worship banner or a quilt hanging for an area in your church. Remember: Whatever we do that is *all about him* is worship.

Chapter 1: Think about the Ten Commandments without referring to your Bible. Do you remember what they are? Do you remember the first four from Exodus 20:3–11?

> 1. *You must not have any other god but me.*
> 2. *You must not make for yourself an idol of any kind. . . .*
>   *You must not bow down to them or worship them, for I, the LORD your God, am a jealous God who will not tolerate your affection for any other gods. . . .*
> 3. *You must not misuse the name of the LORD your God. . . .*
> 4. *Remember to observe the Sabbath day by keeping it holy.*

The first four commandments are devoted to worship. They are all about him. Before discussing chapter 1, ask members of the group to think about their own worship; then as a group discuss how the first four commandments should influence how we worship today. What is God telling us about himself?

Chapter 2: When we think of how we worship God, our minds usually think immediately of our worship service. Worshiping with other Christians is critical to a committed life with God—but what about personal, one-on-One worship? In this session, encourage members to enlarge their thinking when it comes to worship, to move away from compartmentalizing it and instead incorporating it into their day-to-day life. This chapter lists five ways to worship. Ask members to suggest other ways to worship that we don't always think of as worship. For example, sharing our resources with others can be a form of worship, whether it's through tithing or bringing a casserole to a family in need.

Chapter 3: It's harder to do practically everything—sometimes *anything!*—when you're suffering, and it's particularly hard to worship God when we know that if he chose to, he could relieve our crisis. But there are a few things we need to remember before we get too far down that road. Consider opening the session by leading a discussion about what may be helpful as the group tackles this tough subject. You might ask some of the following questions:

- Does God ask us how we feel about worshiping him? (Reference last week's discussion of the Ten Commandments.)

- Can we worship despite our feelings or only when we're feeling loving toward God?

- Can worship ever be a sacrifice or offering to God?

- Have any in the group gone through a time of suffering and come out the other side, seeing how God used that sad season to bring something of value to their lives? What was that experience?

- Does the act of worship ever change our hearts and feelings?

- While this study focuses on Jeremiah, it goes without saying that Job is synonymous with suffering. Consider asking a member of the group to study Job's responses to his own suffering and how that did or did not impact how he worshiped the Lord.

Chapter 4: Revelation has a lot to teach us about worship because it describes worship in heaven. Is there a better template than that? Chapters 4 and 5 are among the more accessible, and they describe more than a dozen different actions that comprise the worship that takes place in heaven. Ask your group to focus on the forms of worship that include these Scriptures and then to discuss ways we might emulate them here on earth. "Worthy is the Lamb!"

EVERYDAY MATTERS BIBLE STUDIES
for women

Spiritual practices for everyday life

Acceptance	Mentoring
Bible Study & Meditation	Outreach
Celebration	Prayer
Community	Reconciliation
Confession	Sabbath & Rest
Contemplation	Service
Faith	Silence
Fasting	Simplicity
Forgiveness	Solitude
Gratitude	Stewardship
Hospitality	Submission
Justice	Worship

HENDRICKSON PUBLISHERS

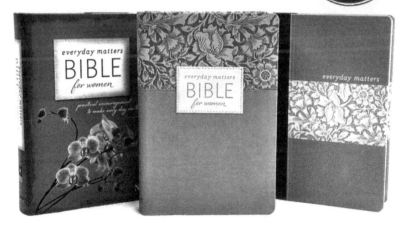